PRAISE FOR LYNETTE YETTER'S

72 MONEY SAVING TIPS FOR THE 99%

"As co-founder of a socially-concerned company, I whole-heartedly endorse Lynette Yetter's book *72 Money Saving Tips for the 99%.* This book is not just one, but many steps in the right direction. It is full of surprising secrets of human happiness -- told with wit and humor."

- Jerry Greenfield, Ben & Jerry's Ice Cream

"*72 Money Saving Tips for the 99%* is the indigenous anti-crisis plan."

- Yorokobu Magazine (Spain)

"This book is more than a compilation of practical money-saving tips, though many of the suggestions are very doable. It's an invitation to think beyond our consumption-driven lifestyle and find a simpler way of being. Yetter is inspired by the ancient lifeways of Andean farmers, which survive today as models of living in harmony with the earth. She also includes insights from Buddhism and quotes from a variety of well-known thinkers such as Henry David Thoreau. The book is an enjoyable invitation to rethink our daily existence."

- Dr. Maya Stanfield Mazzi, University of Florida

"It's Handy Heloise's Tips for the alternatives."

- Dr. Rantu Press

I0039700

"A perfect bathroom book!"

- Liz Baldwin, Massachusetts, USA

"Being from the 60's . . . (*72 Money Saving Tips for the 99%*) is right up my alley of books I want on my shelf. It has useful information and recipes for soap and cosmetics and is in a charming format. Not bogged down with a lot of filler. It is also easy to gift."

- Carolynn Benson Smithson-Grant, Indiana, USA

"A great guide that explains how to live in harmony with Pachamama."

- Katey Linkous, Mount Hood, Oregon

OTHER WORKS BY LYNETTE YETTER

Lucy Plays Panpipes for Peace, a novel

Nam Myoho Renge Kyo (music video)

Espiritu Incaico/Inka Spirit (music CD)

Music of the Andes and More (music CD)

www.LynetteYetter.com

72 Money-Saving Tips

for the 99%

By Lynette Yetter

LynetteYetter.com

Portland, Oregon 2013

Published by Lynette Yetter and LynetteYetter.com
Portland, Oregon
sales@lynetteyetter.com

Printed in the United States of America.

Cover art and layout by Lynette Yetter

Portions of this book were previously published on www.blogcritics.org and www.lynetteyetter.com.

Distributed by Ingram

Library of Congress Control Number: 2012910451

Yetter, Lynette, 1959-

72 Money-Saving Tips for the 99%

/ by Lynette Yetter.--Second U.S. ed.

p. cm. -

"Lynette Yetter and LynetteYetter.com"

ISBN-10 0-9843756-5-1 (pbk. : alk. paper)

ISBN-13 978-0-9843756-5-3

1. Globalization - Economic aspects. 2. Indigenous Peoples - Andes. 3. Finance - Personal - United States. 4. Social reform. I. Title: Money saving tips for the 99%. II. Title: Money saving tips for the ninety nine percent. III. Title: Money saving tips for the 99 percent. IV. Title.

Second U.S. Edition, paperback 2013

Printed on Sustainable Forestry Initiative® (SFI®) Certified Sourcing paper.

For

all people of courage, compassion and wisdom

throughout the past, present and future.

Table of Contents

Acknowledgments

In the spirit of turning poison into medicine, I thank life for providing difficulties -- for the difficulties are what spur me to seek and learn. I thank my mentors and friends on this journey of life, especially my parents who continue to teach me in unexpected ways even though they have passed on. Thank you Paul Barnett and Elvia Jove for reading a draft of this book and giving your feedback. Thank you Liz Baldwin for giving feedback on portions of this book. Thank you Jill Elliott for your gift of editing. Thank you biologist Emily Reddington-Harris for fact-checking. Thank you Reed College librarians. Thank you Daisaku Ikeda, my mentor in life, for encouraging me that nothing is impossible and that we can create a happier, more just future for all living beings on our magnificent blue orb. Thank you Smokey, for sharing this journey of life together.

Thank you everyone who has crossed my path, for you have each taught me something just by being you.

Thank you, Dear Reader, for sharing your time with me in this book.

"To change oneself now is to change the future on a vast scale."

- Daisaku Ikeda

(page 14, Planetary Citizenship)

Introduction

BACKGROUND

In this introduction I give you a "peek behind the scenes" into my thoughts that are the foundation upon which these 72 money saving tips rest.

The tips in this book are things I have done, seen other people doing, or read about and embrace as good ideas.

Having lived for years off-the-grid in a school bus in California, then with indigenous people in the roadless mountains of Nicaragua and in the *altiplano* of Peru and Bolivia, I find that people have been living very economically for as long as anyone can remember, and being happy in the process. Living in Latin America opened my eyes to the fact that most of the world lives with far less material consumption than most folks in the US. It became obvious that happiness has nothing to do with being a consumer and striving to have a certain lifestyle.

HOW TO READ THIS BOOK

You can open the book at random and find a cheerfully presented money-saving tip to instruct, ponder or entertain --

depending on your point of view. The tips are in no particular order, so you can flip through the book at your whim.

Some tips are simple while others are more complex. The simple tips you can do right now. The more complex tips I introduce as a general idea; I often list a website and/or book that you can read for more detailed information.

I write the tips with tongue in cheek and a light heart. Before each tip is a thought-provoking quote from thinkers like Thoreau, Booker T. Washington, Daisaku Ikeda and others -- people who like to put their hands in the earth and learn to live in equilibrium.

I find inspiration in the words of Daisaku Ikeda, " . . . Create a diverse, cooperative . . . society. To this end, each individual must change the models of his or her actions." (page 72, *Planetary Citizenship*).

What models can we look towards? In many of the money saving tips I look to the wisdom of our indigenous ancestors who have lived sustainably for thousands of years. And I look to the creativity of people everywhere who are finding ways to save money while being happy living a simpler life -- people who are concerned not just for their own personal comfort, but for the happiness and well-being of all life.

THOUGHTS

Although I wrote the tips in an upbeat chatty tone, (somewhat like you might find in a mainstream women's magazine) the money saving tips I present are out of the ordinary. Some may even find them a bit shocking. One thing most of the tips have in common is that they do not benefit big business -- they do not benefit the richest 1% of the people.

As a member of the 99% I am attracted to time-tested ways of living simply -- in harmony with our human species and with Pachamama, our Mother Earth.

For example, although occasionally I do buy used clothes, I do not list this as a money saving tip. Why? Because it is not sustainable. Living off the dregs of globalized capitalism is not something that can continue for the next 10,000 years. A more sustainable tip would be what Gandhi and his followers did -- spin our own fiber and make our own clothes. Now that is something that is liberating -- liberating us from reliance on Big Business. It worked for Gandhi to help liberate the entire country of India. Perhaps it can work for us, the 99%.

Some of the tips point towards strengthening community with our neighbors. This is powerful. In fact, in Naomi Klein's book *The Shock Doctrine* she documented small local groups of people unified for their common good who stood up to big business, and won.

A FEW WORDS ABOUT ANIMALS AND PLANTS

A vegetarian friend strongly objected to the tips in this book that deal with raising animals for meat and leather. She sent me an article about boys glorifying in killing a chicken for sport. She questioned how killing an animal could possibly contribute to world peace. Perhaps you have the same question.

Here's one way to look at it -- Shakyamuni Buddha is quoted as saying, "We can kill the desire to kill."

The thoughts and emotions we embrace in our mind and heart are the crux of the matter. Do we see ourselves as separate from the natural world (like the boys who were cruel to a chicken)? Or do we see ourselves as a microcosm of everything -- that we are all one?

If we embrace the latter viewpoint, then we are more in harmony with these words of 13th century Buddhist reformer Nichiren Daishonin: "Life at each moment encompasses the body and mind and the self and environment of all sentient beings . . . as well as all insentient beings, including plants, sky, earth, and even the minutest particles of dust." (Writings of Nichiren Daishonin, page 3)

Nurturing in our hearts this awareness of oneness of all life, it would be impossible to torture an animal. Also, even while eating a salad we could deepen our awareness of the sensations of the living beings we call lettuce leaves, and empathize. When I saw the movie based on the book *The Secret Life of Plants,* I became abruptly aware that plants feel and have awareness.

. . . AND APPLES AND ORANGES

This same friend also observed that the tips in this book are like comparing apples and oranges. That's exactly right. Indigenous thought can be said to be like apples -- organic apples. And Western Industrialized Society thought is like oranges -- navel oranges.

Of course these metaphors are not perfect. No metaphor is.

Continuing with this metaphor, we can eat an organic apple. It nourishes us. And in its core are seeds. The seeds can grow into apple trees to produce more apples for us to eat.

Apples are sustainable, like indigenous cultures that have lived in balance with Mother Earth -- Pachamama -- for thousands of years.

Navel oranges, especially ones found in a supermarket produce section, are big and colorful. They are conveniently easy to peel. After we eat them they are gone. They have no seeds to plant to grow another navel orange tree.

Navel oranges are not sustainable, like Western Industrialized Society that creates big colorful conveniences, yet also causes global climate change, logarithmically expanding population growth and depletion of non-renewable natural resources from our Mother. The petroleum to fuel our cars and metals to make batteries to power our Prius's will not regenerate if planted like apple seeds. When non-renewable natural resources are gone, like navel oranges they are gone.

The point of these tips is to show sustainable ways that people are, or have been, living. Sustainable like the organic apples mentioned above. And to illustrate that Western Industrialized Society's non-sustainable consumer (navel orange) lifestyle is not the only way to live. In fact, many people of Western Industrialized Society are dying -- if not from cancer caused by the pollutants corporations have dumped into the environment, then increasingly by suicide as hope dwindles.

There is hope. There *are* different ways to think and to live. I hope that the ideas in this book will be like delicious organic apples whose seeds sprout as part of a new garden of mutually beneficial sustainable life.

WHERE?

Where did I write this book? The first draft I wrote in Bolivia. The final draft I wrote in Portland, Oregon where I had the opportunity to participate in the Occupy Movement.

The Occupy Movement has popularized Howard Zinn's phrase "The 99%." It is we, the 99% (together with our Mother Sun and Earth) who provide the wealth for 1% of the human race.

These money-saving tips for the 99% are 72 ways to save hard-earned cash instead of giving it to corporations that make the rich richer and the poor poorer.

Naomi Klein documents other strategies in her book *No Logo.* There, she notes how student and other activist groups have pressured transnational corporations to be a bit more humanistic by threatening to take their business to other companies.

The tips in this book are not about which company we buy from. They are more in harmony with the DIY ethic of Booker T. Washington. In his autobiography *Up From Slavery,* he tells how he encouraged the students of Tuskegee Institute to build their own school, starting with digging the clay to form the bricks they laid. Instead of being consumers for the profit of the 1%, we, in the words of Booker T. Washington, can "Learn to love work for its own sake."

This reminds me of the Gees Bend Quilt Show I saw at the DeYoung Museum in San Francisco, California. There were video interviews with the women who had made the quilts. One quilter talked about how when the Great Depression hit they didn't notice any difference because they had been dirt-poor to begin with. In that era she, like all the women in Gees Bend, rose before dawn to cook for her family. Then they walked to the cotton fields and worked all day. On the way home, if she found a scrap of a rag on the ground, she picked it up, took it home and washed it to use in a quilt. After cooking dinner for the family and getting everyone to bed, the women gathered together to quilt. As they quilted, they sang long into the night.

She commented that even though people now have a lot more things, those things don't bring happiness. Her happiest times were when she had nothing but the bare minimum, plus lots of friendship and love.

My hope is that some of these money saving tips will spark ideas in you -- ideas of how to create more of your own happiest times, with friendship and love.

- Lynette Yetter, Portland, Oregon, June 2012

"Enjoy the simple, the natural and the plain. Along with that comes the ability to do things spontaneously and have them work."

- Benjamin Hoff

TIP #1

Cut up old cotton clothes instead of using sanitary-napkins or tampons

That's right. Save money. Don't buy any more tampons or sanitary napkins! That's what I'm doing. Actually I got the idea from my step mom, who grew up on a farm in Indiana. She said that is what they used. Plus, you are protecting the environment by not adding more garbage to the world.

"The best things in life aren't things."

- Art Buchwald

TIP #2

Sell your washing machine at a garage sale

Save money on your electric bill. Don't throw those bloody strips of cloth (from Tip #1) into the washer machine. Wash them by hand. At first it kind of grossed me out. But I got over it. Wash all your clothes by hand! That's what most of us do, here in the Andes.

The rag I spread out on the drain board next to the sink. I use a block of locally made soap. No colorants or deodorants. Just lard and lye and I don't know if there are any other ingredients. It is the beige color of animal fat and has a bit of that earthy aroma.

With the soap I use a scrub brush, like I saw my neighbor using. I rub the brush over the bar of soap then dip it in water (cold, or warmed in the sun. Save yet more money on gas and electric bills!)

and scrub away. I scrub in the direction of the sink, so the spatters mainly end up there ready to get rinsed down the drain.

The neighbor, who taught me the scrub brush technique, uses a chemical laundry detergent. It is packed with environment-killing phosphates that were long ago banned in the States. So, the companies started exporting them to the Third World.

The soap idea I learned from a rural family in Nicaragua, with whom I lived for some time. They told me they had used a fruit from a certain tree that lathers up, much like the Soap Root native to the central coast of California. But, with US-style consumerism being promoted worldwide, that rural family started buying soap.

In the countryside in Nicaragua, we washed our clothes on rocks in the river. They had a special rock that was flat and angled into the water. You spread each item of wet clothing, one at a time, on the rock. Then you rub a bar of soap all over the surface of the clothing. Then grab a wad of the bottom of the clothing, and pin down the top with your other hand, and scrub. Every now and then you pour water over the item of clothing. And scrub some more.

Washing by hand is good exercise. Save yet more money because you won't need to go to the gym or an exercise class. Get your work-out the natural way; labor with your hands.

"Beauty of style and harmony and grace and good rhythm depend on simplicity."

– Plato

Tip #3

Don't buy new underwear

Did you know that underwear is a recent invention? That's right. Check it out for yourself. Google "history" and "underwear" and see what you find.

Traditional indigenous women here in the Andes often don't use underwear. It is a very practical habit. When you have the urge to urinate, you just poosh out your big skirts like a tent and squat in the field or the street or where ever. Guys no longer have a monopoly on using the world as their urinal.

You save money! No more dreaded "panty lines"! As your old cotton underwear falls apart, you can cut it up and use it for when you are "on the rag."

"You have succeeded in life when all you really want is only what you really need."

- Vernon Howard

TIP #4

Trade in your car for a bicycle and cash

I have seen people here in Bolivia carting heavy sacks of potatoes looped over the top bar of their bicycle.

No more car insurance bills. No more buying gas. No more repair bills. You get lots of exercise which lowers cholesterol, blood pressure and improves health. Lower health care expenses. Save money and protect non-renewable resources.

"Unnecessary possessions are unnecessary burdens.

If you have them, you have to take care of them!

There is great freedom in simplicity of living. It is

those who have enough but not too much

who are the happiest."

- Peace Pilgrim

TIP #5

Get rid of cable and TV

Without advertising propaganda infiltrating your brain, you will bit by bit free yourself of the addiction to buy and consume more than you need. You will save money by not paying for cable, or for the electricity to run the TV, or fixing it. Sell your TV and get instant cash!

For more info you can check out the books *Propaganda* by Edward Bernays and *Four Arguments For the Elimination of Television* by Jerry Mander.

"We don't need to increase our goods nearly as much as we need to scale down our wants. Not wanting something is as good as possessing it."

- Donald Horba

TIP #6

Stop buying air freshener

Save money and protect your health. Those air freshener sprays are laden with chemicals that harm you and the environment from start to finish. Instead, pick some flowers from that community garden you'll create with your neighbors (See Tip #21). Or ask your kid to run over and pick the flowers. More exercise for a growing body and mind!

The natural floral scent will freshen the room. And flowers are a lot more beautiful to look at than a can that will go into the garbage and then into landfills that won't be healthy for Pachamama for many, many years. When the flowers wilt and get slimy, add them to your compost and they will soon be nutrition for next year's flowers!

And to really clean the air, potted plants work great. Get a cutting from a friend, some dirt from outside, and a pot can be any old container. Place in a sunny spot and just add water. Potted plants suck out volatile organic compounds (VOCs) from the air in your home. And that's a good thing.

"Tis a gift to be simple, tis a gift to be free . . ."

- Joseph Brackett Jr.

TIP #7

Take a Walk

Want to spend quality time with your loved one and save money? Take a walk together. Enjoy the sites. Talk. No expensive restaurants. No expensive movie theatres. Side by side you walk and talk and connect heart to heart. Walking and companionship are great for improving health. Walking can also lower your health care bills!

"To simplify complications is the first essential of success."

- George Earle Buckle

TIP #8

Use a re-usable bag to carry your purchases

Throwing away or recycling plastic or paper bags adds to the costs of dealing with our waste. As more people use a re-usable bag, trash bills drop, and we express more appreciation for our dear Mother Earth who keeps us alive.

My favorite way to carry my groceries is like the Aymara and Quechua woman in Bolivia -- in a *qhepi*. A *qhepi* is a cloth-wrapped bundle on your back tied around your shoulders.

"The ordinary arts we practice every day at home are of more importance to the soul than their simplicity might suggest."

- Thomas Moore

TIP #9

Get rid of your water heater

Your money gets eaten up minute by minute as a traditional water heater maintains the temperature of a tank of water, whether you are using it or not. You can replace your water heater with an on-demand shower head water heater. Electric shower heads run from $2 - $15 and are available at many mom-and-pop hardware stores in Bolivia. Take short hot showers, so you don't run up your electricity bill, or water bill.

"The sculptor produces the beautiful statue by chipping away such parts of the marble block as are not needed – it is a process of elimination."

- Elbert Hubbard

TIP #10

Heat water in the sun

Some friends in Puno, Peru taught me to use wide dark buckets to heat water in the sun. Their only water source is a hose bib in the yard. And the town only has running water for the first few hours of the day. So, first thing in the morning they run a hose to fill up a bunch of these buckets. After sitting in the *altiplano* sunlight for awhile, the water warms up. To bathe, dip a washcloth in the water and bathe near a bucket in the yard. Or use a pitcher to pour the water over your head for washing your hair.

Another friend uses two large dark-colored plastic bowls for washing dishes. Both of the bowls she fills with water and sets them on a bench in the sunlight. One bowl is the wash water and the second bowl is the rinse water.

In the US I saw this DIY set-up: Get an old water heater. Paint it black. Put it on the roof where it will bake in the sun. The folks I saw using this built a flared-open box for the tank to rest in on its side. The box they also painted black. Connect black tubes to it.

Save money by using less water and heating with the warmth of Tata Inti, the sun.

"Progress is man's ability to complicate simplicity."

- Thor Heyerdahl

TIP #11

Catch rain water

Some friends of mine in Bolivia put 55 gallon metal drums under their down spouts. A hanging chain directs the water into the drum where it collects and can be used to water the garden, wash clothes or dishes, or boiled for drinking.

Save money on your water bill by placing a barrel under your downspout.

"Most of the luxuries, and many of the so-called comforts of life, are not only not indispensable, but positive hindrances to the elevation of mankind. With respect to luxuries and comforts, the wisest have even lived a more simple and meagre life than the poor."

- Henry David Thoreau

TIP #12

Clean with hot water instead of chemicals

You save money by not buying cleaning products. I boil up a kettle of hot water and pour it over the toilet after scrubbing it out with a brush. Boiling water has been a time-tested antibacterial for thousands of years. You save money by not buying cleaning products. And your health is protected by not having possible cancer-causing chemicals in the house.

"If your mind isn't clouded by unnecessary things, this is the best season of your life."

- Wu-Men

TIP #13

Use old clothes as rags

You don't need to buy Swifter covers or special Handiwipes or anything. Just use an old t-shirt, or some other old clothing with a high content of natural fibers (cotton seems to work best). For damp mopping the floor, here in Bolivia we flop a damp t-shirt over the end of an old mop, or any pole with a crosspiece on one end. It could even be a branch from a tree! Push that damp t-shirt around the floor with the pole. Rinse out and squeeze the t-shirt in a bucket of water, then swish it around some more.

What other cleaning uses can you come up with for old clothes?

"I am beginning to learn that it is the sweet, simple things in life which are the real ones after all."

- Laura Ingalls Wilder

TIP #14

Sell your vacuum cleaner and cut the rug

Instant cash! Get rid of wall-to-wall carpeting. Or better yet, cut that old wall-to-wall carpet into pieces small enough for you to lift and carry by yourself (instant throw-rugs!). You won't need to maintain a vacuum cleaner or buy vacuum cleaner bags. And will save money on your electric bill. Plus you get more exercise shaking out the throw-rugs and beating them. (While beating the rugs, wear a damp cloth over your nose and mouth so you don't inhale the dust).

Saves you money on gym bills and health care bills, with all this exercise you'll be getting. Be sure to stretch well before and after!

"Live simply that others might simply live."

- Elizabeth Seaton

TIP #15

Resole your Crocs with tire tread

Make your shoes last longer! Resole your shoes using old tires and Barge Cement. (Be sure to not breathe the fumes. Working outside is best). Go to a local garage where they sell tires and ask them to give you an old tire that they would have to pay someone to dispose of anyway. Take the tire home and, trial and error, figure out how many uses you can get out of that tire. Here in the Andes many families make their living resoling shoes, making bungee cords, laundry basins and even shoes themselves, all out of old tires that would have gone to a landfill. The first people to make these items didn't have anyone to show them how to do it. They just used their imagination and kept at it until they figured it out. You can, too! And once you are confident resoling your own shoes, you can even offer this service to your friends and neighbors. So, you not only save money on footwear, but you may create a completely new income stream!

My "everyday" Crocs are now about six years old and on their second resole, expertly done by a friend in Puno, Peru. How many years can you make your shoes last, by resoling them with old tires?

For more info you can see a photo online of my Crocs re-soled with a Michelin tire at http://blogcritics.org/culture/article/three-money-saving-tips1/.

"Our life is frittered away by detail... Simplify, simplify."

- Henry Thoreau

TIP #16

Let your hair grow

Be in solidarity with indigenous people.

No more money spent on haircuts. The last time I cut my hair was in 1983.

"Simplicity in character, in manners, in style; in all things the supreme excellence is simplicity."

- Henry Wadsworth Longfellow

TIP #17

Let your hair be the way it wants to be

No more money spent of hair dye, perms, streaks, gels, hairspray, etc. Is your hair curly? Let it be curly! Is it straight? Let it be straight! Is it gray? You guessed it, let it be gray.

Save money by being yourself!

"Simplicity is indeed often the sign of truth and a criterion of beauty."

- Mahlon Hoagland

TIP #18

Style your hair the indigenous way

Many women in Peru and Bolivia braid their hair in two braids. The ends are fastened by braiding a string in, then tying the string at the end. No more money spent on hair ties, clips, bands, etc.

Amazingly enough, when you braid your hair this way, the ends do not split. No need for trims. And women tell me that by braiding my hair it will grow longer faster. I can hardly wait!

Men sometimes tie their tresses in a ponytail with a string.

"Making the simple complicated is commonplace;
making the complicated simple, awesomely simple,
that's creativity."

- Charles Mingus

TIP #19

Use white cotton rags instead of band aids

Got a little cut or owie? Grab a strip of those old clothes that you have sterilized by boiling, and tie it around your finger, or where ever you need to. Stops the bleeding and keeps the wound clean to heal quickly. No more money spent on band aids!

"As you simplify your life, the laws of the universe will be simpler; solitude will not be solitude, poverty will not be poverty, nor weakness weakness."

- Henry David Thoreau

TIP #20

Watch DVDs on your computer

Of course, if you do not have a computer, this tip does not apply. But if you do have a computer, you can consolidate.

Sell your TV and DVD player at a garage sale and get instant cash. And you will not need to pay money to maintain or replace a separate device or devices to watch movies.

"Anything simple always interests me."

- David Hockney

TIP #21

Share with your neighbors

Start a small urban/suburban farm.

Communal land has been fundamental in the Andean Cosmovision, as it has been with all of our ancestors from the dawning of humanity. In times of need, we remember this. Like during WWII when people in San Francisco, California tore down their backyard fences and made whole blocks into giant community gardens.

Trading the produce with each other, everyone has a balanced diet and enough to eat.

For more info you can check out the organic gardening books by Eliot Coleman. One of my favorite parts is the section on Deep Organics in *The Winter Harvest Handbook.*

"Nothing is more simple than greatness; indeed, to be simple is to be great."

- Ralph Waldo Emerson

TIP #22

Dig your own ditch

Have your neighborhood association petition the city to allow you and your neighbors to labor on local public works projects.

For example, in my neighborhood in Bolivia we all got out our picks and shovels; together we dug a trench for replacing our water main with a wider diameter pipe. First we pried up the paving stones, then dug up the road. That night the city plumber replaced the pipe. The next day we put the road back together.

Lower taxes! More exercise for better health, thereby lowering health care bills!

"Simplicity, clarity, singleness: These are the attributes that give our lives power and vividness and joy as they are also the marks of great art."

- Richard Holloway

TIP #23

Use cloth diapers instead of disposable

Whether for babies or anyone with bladder-control issues, save money by not buying disposable diapers. You save at the checkout stand and you save in the long run by not polluting with yet more garbage, or supporting plastics industries that by their very nature pollute.

When I was a little girl I remember that the baby sitter washed cloth diapers by first soaking them in the toilet bowl to remove the solid matter. It's yucky at the moment, but your air will be cleaner, the climate will be more stable, you have a chance to be healthier, and you save money!

"Simplicity is the key to brilliance."

- Bruce Lee

TIP #24

Freeze dry

When I was a kid in California, freeze dried food was "space age." It was what the Apollo astronauts ate. Little did I know that freeze drying food is a technology developed by our ancestors thousands of years ago, and still practiced in the traditional ways in the Andes. One of the most common freeze dried foods in Bolivia is *chuñu.*

If you live in a climate where it gets below freezing, you don't need anything except potatoes, freezing nights, and clean feet.

Here's how I was told to do it: Peel the potatoes. Set them outside on a freezing night. In the morning let them defrost in the daylight. Then stomp out the moisture from the thawed potatoes and let them dry in the sun.

"Life is beautiful in its simplicity."

- Thomas Matthiessen

TIP #24

Can

You can preserve your own food -- those vegetables you yourself grew in a community garden. No longer are chemicals from the adhesives in metal commercial cans getting into your food. And since you grew the food yourself (hopefully organically), you know it is not full of chemicals and pesticides. Also you save money by not paying all those hidden costs of shipping and trucking canned goods halfway around the world. Your conscience also rests easier because the food you are eating you labored for with your own hands in the soil of our Mother Earth; it was not a product of some big corporation profiting from the under-paid labor of people in the Third World. Your health can improve since you are eating better quality food. So you can even save money in the long run on medical bills!

And best of all, the food tastes better!

Get some jars, rubber gaskets and airtight lids, then boil them to sterilize them. For step-by-step canning instructions you can visit the websites http://pickyourown.org/allaboutcanning.htm or http://nchfp.uga.edu/how/can_home.html. Or better yet, find someone in your neighborhood who knows how to can and learn from her.

You may just make a new friend!

"Simplicity is making the journey of this life with just baggage enough."

- Charles Dudley Warner

TIP #25

Dehydrate

Here in the altiplano the air is so dry that things just dehydrate all on their own. To make *charque* (what some folks call jerky), we just cut thin slices of meat, rub salt on them and hang them over a clothesline to dry.

"Simplicity and naturalness are the truest marks of distinction."

- W. Somerset Maugham

TIP #26

Get a Pig

Feed you kitchen scraps to your pig. Less garbage! With lots of people doing this over time, garbage collection fees drop. Your pig can be like a guard dog for when you are away. Porky can provide you with other things, too.

Read the next couple of Tips to find out more.

"Grandeur and beauty are so very opposite, that you often diminish the one as you increase the other. Variety is most akin to the latter, simplicity to the former."

- William Shenstone

TIP #27

Eat your pig

Home butchering is getting more popular. Did you know that pigs are said to be the most nutritious meat animals? Oh my! Now my stomach is turning, thinking of killing one of our cousin creatures. It reminds me that one night I slept next to a recently slaughtered pig in Peru. His mate had screamed as he was slaughtered.

But a couple of days later, when he was cooked up and served to all us panpipe players (sikuris), we somehow forgot the sadness of the pig's death and enjoyed the succulent meal.

If you want, here is a website with step-by-step directions of how to butcher a pig: http://www.motherearthnews.com/Sustainable-Farming/1982-09-01/An-Old-Fashioned-Hog-Slaughter.aspx

"Simple pleasures are the last healthy refuge in a complex world."

- Oscar Wilde

TIP #28

Wear your pig

Leather. The material with 101 uses. Make gloves or shoes or jackets or even footballs from the skin of your pig.

When I lived with a family in the roadless mountains of Nicaragua, they showed me a creekside basin their ancestors had carved in the bedrock using a machete. That basin was where my friends had observed their grandparents tanning hides using materials they gathered from the wild. "What materials?" I asked. They did not know. Western Industrialized Society's chemicals came to their area, and their use erased that ancestral wisdom.

But, you could be that ancestor who starts a new branch of wisdom to pass along. And you save money in the process!

For more info on turning your pig skin into leather you can check out http://tech.groups.yahoo.com/group/PasturedPigs/.

"Nature is what we know – Yet have not art to say –

So impotent our wisdom is to her simplicity."

- Emily Dickinson

TIP #29

Get a Goat

Goat's milk cheese -- yum! Not only will your goat squirt out dairy products (some assembly required), but she will also clip your grass for free. You can even rent her out to eat the weeds on someone else's land. And when her lifetime is over, her skin makes a great drum head. That is what we stretch over our *bombo* drums in the Andean *altiplano* -- goat hides.

"But what about the cheese?" you may ask. Here's a simple cheese recipe from the book *Caprine Supply's Goatkeeping 101; Sensible Information From People Who Know and Raise Goats*:

1. Slowly heat a gallon of goat milk to 185°F, using a stainless steel or enamelware pot.
2. Add 1/4 cup vinegar.
3. Keep the temperature at 185°F, stirring the milk occasionally, for 10 to 15 minutes. At this point a soft curd should form.
4. Line a colander or strainer with cheesecloth.

5. Pour the curd into the colander, and sprinkle the curd with salt.
6. Tie the corners of the cloth together.
7. Hang it to drip for a few hours.
8. Eat the cheese immediately, or refrigerate it for up to a week.

"Simplicity involves unburdening your life, and living more lightly with fewer distractions that interfere with a high quality life, as defined uniquely by each individual. You will find people living simply in large cities, rural areas and everything in between."

- Linda Breen Pierce

TIP #30

Get a sheep

Wool keeps you warm even when it is wet.

You can sell the wool to people who knit or weave. Or you can card it and spin it yourself. That's what Gandhi and his followers did with cotton -- made their own clothes. And with that process (and others) they gained their freedom.

For more info on preparing wool you can check out http://finance.groups.yahoo.com/group/GoatandSheepRancher/ and http://www.joyofhandspinning.com/HowToDropspin.shtml.

For free knitting patterns you can check out http://www.straw.com/cpy/free_patterns.html.

For more info on Gandhi you can check out the book *The Life of Mahatma Gandhi* by Louis Fischer.

"Simplicity is the glory of expression."

- Walt Whitman

TIP #31

Sell your lawn mower

Your goat and/or sheep will keep your lawn trimmed. No gardening service needed, or lawn mower or weed whacker! To make sure the goat or sheep graze where you want her to, and not in your petunia bed, is to do as I've seen in the Andes -- tie a rope around one leg and the other end of the rope to a stake in the ground.

Get instant cash by selling your mower!

"The ability to simplify means to eliminate the unnecessary so that the necessary may speak."

- Hans Hofmann

TIP #32

Never buy fertilizer again

Those little round pellets your sheep excretes are great fertilizer for your garden. Save money and protect your health. Even most "organic" fertilizer you buy at a store is bad for your health; because to produce the plastic bag it is in, and to pack and ship it to your local store, uses up natural resources and adds pollution to the environment. Your sheep's droppings are 100% organic. And what could be more local than fertilizer originating in your very own yard?

"The great artist and thinker is the simplifier."

- Henri Frederic Amiel

TIP #33

Sell your electric coffee grinder at a garage sale

Get instant cash and save money month after month on your electric bill.

Grind your coffee beans between two rocks. It is a tried and tested tool, used for thousands of years. Your rocks can be like a mortar and pestle. Or like the *batáns* we use here in Bolivia. A *batán* is in two parts. The bottom part is a flat rock with a bit of a dip in it. The top part is a crescent shaped stone that you rock back and forth.

Everyone here raves about how everything tastes better when it is ground between rocks.

I agree.

"As I grew older, I realized that it was much better to insist on the genuine forms of nature, for simplicity is the greatest adornment of art."

- Albrecht Durer

TIP #34

Sell your food processor at a garage sale

Get instant cash and save money month after month on your electric bill. You even save time!

Grind your food between two rocks. I'm telling ya -- fresh basil, garlic and nuts grind up into a pesto paste almost faster than you can say, "bon apetite." And everything tastes better when it is ground with rocks. (For rock suggestions, see #33). And the clean up time? Hot water and a rag and whoosh it's clean! Not like the long tinker toy project of disassembling a food processor and cleaning it and putting it back together again.

"Simplicity, clarity, singleness: these are the attributes that give our lives power and vividness and joy."

- Richard Halloway

TIP #35

Sell your dishwasher at a garage sale

Get instant cash and save money on your electric bill and water bill every month.

Wash your dishes by hand. I wash most of my dishes in cold water. For dishes that are greasy, I heat up water on the stove. A friend of mine uses two shallow buckets to wash her dishes. She fills them both with water and sets them in the sun to warm up. One is the wash bucket, the other the rinse. She saves the most money of all! No heating water on a stove. Absolute minimum of water used. Wow! What are you going to use the money on, that you'll get by selling your dishwasher?

Here's a little poem, "Ode to Dishwater." *Rain of dishwater / cast from the neighbor's kitchen window above / glistens in the east-born sunbeams / slanting from Illimani's glaciered peaks. / Spatter patter. / The dishwater, / like an intermittent cascade, / embraces the dry clay soil / in the garden below -- / merging in cool dampness.*

"Simplicity of character is the natural result of profound thought."

- William Hazlitt

TIP #36

Stop buying dish detergent

Use a bar of soap and a rag. It's much cheaper, more gentle on the environment and better for your health. You save cash immediately; and your health care costs might lower because of less chemicals and plastic in the world. You are making our planet a healthier place to live.

"Purity and simplicity are the two wings with which man soars above the earth and all temporary nature."

- Thomas Kempis

TIP #37

Stop buying laundry detergent

You already sold your washing machine (see Tip #2) and are washing your clothes by hand. Using a bar of soap instead of laundry detergent is cheaper and better for your health and the health of the planet.

"Enjoy the little things, for one day you may look back and realize they were the big things."

- Robert Brault

TIP #38

Stay Warm Cheap

Turn off the heater. Here in the Andes, almost no one uses a heater. That's for the rich folks. When it is snowing outside, we put on lots of layers of clothes. However, it doesn't get much below freezing here, since we are so close to the equator.

If you live in a more arctic zone, you can save money the Inuit Way. See next tip.

"From native simplicity we arrive at more profound simplicity."

- Albert Schweitzer

TIP #39

Dig a hole

To save money on heating and stay warm when temperatures drop to minus 100 degrees Fahrenheit or more -- dig a hole. Of course, the hole is best dug in Summer. Plan ahead!

Traditional Inuit houses are big holes in the ground. Line the hole with tree trunks for stability. Cover the hole with a tree trunk roof, about a foot above ground level. Put a single small window in the log wall (yes, above ground level). This window never opens. It is your porch light. Build a loft bed. Light a candle.

The ancestors circa 1950 A.D. used a whale fat lamp with a moss wick, but candles are easier to come by nowadays. *NOTE: The candle must be kept lit 24 hours a day.* This is your sole heat source. The excellent insulation of your Inuit-style house will keep the heat in and let it accumulate. Hang out on your bunk bed, near the ceiling. It will get so toasty warm you can hang out in the nude. Store your perishable food on the floor. It is nature's icebox. To make the front door, dig a tunnel. Make it bend like a drain pipe. The cold will sink in from outside and be trapped in the bend. You will climb up the next part of the tunnel to enter your home at loft bed level where it will be cozy warm.

Save tons of money on your heating bills!

For more info you can check out the book *Four Ways of Being Human* by Gene Lisitzky.

"Simplicity is the essence of happiness."

- Cedric Bledsoe

TIP #40

Sell your patio and lawn furniture at a garage sale

Get instant cash. Sit outside the Andean way - on the ground. Sitting on the ground helps maintain flexibility in your joints and stretches muscles like gentle yoga. Burns a few more calories in the act of sitting down and getting up. Builds muscle. Every little bit helps!

"In character, in manner, in style, in all things, the supreme excellence is simplicity."

- Henry Wadsworth

TIP #41

Do your pedicure with a rock from the garden

No longer will you need to spend money on pumice stones or callous graters. Do like I learned from a Quechua grandmother in Bolivia. When your calluses bother you, sit down on the ground next to a water source and rub your calluses with a rock. Almost any rock will do.

But, wait! There's more! Save money on health care, too! You are protecting your health by not adding more pollution to the world, such as the exhaust of the delivery trucks that bring pedicure equipment to stores. You're avoiding plastic handles or packaging that required destroying an ecosystem and possibly an indigenous culture to get the petroleum to make it. And there's less trash going into landfills.

With a healthier planet, your health will improve, too. You save money at the checkout register by not buying pedicure implements in the first place and you save money on health care in the long run. *You can't beat a rock!*

"Nothing is true, but that which is simple."

- Johann Wolfgang

TIP #43

Go barefoot

Save even more money on footwear. Go barefoot as much as possible. Walking barefoot on the earth (for example, as you garden) activates the acupressure points in your feet -- aiding in improved health. Here in the Andes people have been going barefoot for thousands of years while working in their fields and enjoying long healthy lives.

So, you not only save money on footwear, but on healthcare costs, too!

"The sanctity of life is known to everyone. At the same time, there is universal confusion about the essential meaning of life's sanctity. If the sanctity of life can become a solid touchstone of wisdom for all people, then humankind's destiny to experience war and misery repeatedly can be greatly transformed. It is toward this end that we Nichiren Buddhists are struggling."

- Daisaku Ikeda

TIP #44

Sell your baby's playpen and plastic toys at a garage sale

Dig a hole. Here in the Andes, for countless generations mothers have dug holes in the earth for their babies and toddlers to play in. The mother is working nearby and the children are safe. The children are absorbing the energy of the Pachamama, learning first-hand about our interconnection of life as they touch the soil, fondle pebbles, make friends with insects, inhale the aromas of the earth that sustains our life, sense the warmth of the earth as Tata Inti (Father Sun) pours affection absorbed by the Pachamama.

As renowned nature guide Elizabeth Terwilliger used to say, "A child who learns to love nature will not harm Mother Nature." No more plastic cages full of the destructive energy from the petroleum industry's actions. The Pachamama will thank you. Your descendants will thank you.

"As we believe simplicity contributes to a peaceful life, we have not bought into the utopia promised by consumerism."

- Harry MacLure

Mush Register; The Hindu (Chennai, India); Mar 22, 2010

TIP #45

Use a thermos

Here in the Andes most folks don't have money to spend on extra gas or electricity to heat up water every time we want a cup of coffee, tea or hot chocolate. We boil water and pour it into a thermos. Throughout the day or night we can pour ourselves a cup of hot water without spending an extra *centavo*.

"Life is not complex. We are complex. Life is simple, and the simple thing is the right thing."

- Oscar Wilde

TIP #46

Stop buying Ritalin for your kid

Did you know that a study showed that learning to swim well improved reading and writing skills in ADD-diagnosed children? If you do not have a body of water nearby, maybe other mindful physical exercise will improve your child's focus and calmness. When I lived with a family in the countryside of Nicaragua -- where there are no roads, no electricity, and you hike a mile to get to the river to carry back water -- I noticed that the children were much calmer and more focused. For example, four-year-olds expertly sharpened machetes before going out to climb trees to cut limbs for firewood.

Children are capable of so much more than Western Industrialized Society allows them.

Save money on drug prescriptions and have happier children and a happier you.

For more info you can check out http://blogcritics.org/scitech/article/swimming-vs-ritalin-in-treating-add/.

"Life is beautiful in its simplicity."

- Thomas Matthiessen

TIP #47

Sell your iPhone and some other electronic gadgets at a garage sale

I find that my laptop with internet connection is about all I need for keeping connected in our global village and doing my work.

No phone. Skype does the job (except for emergency calls).

No extra gadgets for playing music or playing games.

Speaking of playing games -- I prefer a walk in the sunshine or a nap instead of playing a game, whether solitary or interactive. To interact with friends I prefer corresponding or phone calls or best of all, personal visits.

Get extra cash. Less gizmos to worry about can reduce stress. Less stress equals better health and well-being. And you are protecting our Mother by less mining and transportation of non-renewable metals and petroleum.

"Simplicity is the peak of civilization."

- Jessie Sampter

TIP #48

Bathe in a river

You can do like my friends in Nicaragua -- walk to a stream and bathe in running water. They placed a curved strip of bark to direct the water into a little waterfall that makes an excellent shower. Our walks together were great exercise and a chance to enjoy each other's company and admire ever-changing nature. Improves physical and emotional well-being. Also saves money with reduced doctors' bills and helps eliminates the need for antidepressants.

"I have just three things to teach: simplicity, patience, compassion. These three are your greatest treasures."

- Lao Tzu

TIP #49

Bathe in a bucket

One money saving bathing solution is to set a wide bucket of water in the sun. Stand in the sunlight to bathe outside with a washcloth and a bar of soap. Use a pitcher to pour water over your head to wash your hair. This is what lots of us do in the Andes.

"Clutter and confusion are failures of design, not attributes of information."

- Edward Tuft

TIP #50

Don't buy oven cleaner

Expensive and toxic. To clean extra-greasy ovens, according to HealthyChild.org, mix together 1 cup baking soda and 1/4 cup of washing soda, then add enough water to make a paste. Apply the paste to oven surfaces and let soak overnight. The next morning, lift off soda mixture and grime. Then rinse surfaces well.

Or, if you have a bottle of Coca Cola sitting around, it is an excellent corrosive for cleaning ovens and grills. Better to use it to clean your oven than to drink it and destroy your health!

"A great human revolution deep in the heart of a single individual can change the course of human history."

- Daisaku Ikeda (paraphrased)

TIP #51

Don't buy any more glue sticks

Make your own paste from white flour and water.

Ingredients

- 1/2 Cup Flour
- 2 cups Cold Water
- Peppermint Oil

Slowly mix the flour into water. Simmer on low heat and stir constantly until it boils. After it cools you can mix in one or two drops of peppermint oil. This is a natural preservative and it even tastes good! Yum!

"To find the universal elements enough; to find the air and the water exhilarating; to be refreshed by a morning walk or an evening saunter ... to be thrilled by the stars at night; to be elated over a bird's nest or a wildflower in spring—these are some of the rewards of the simple life."

- John Burroughs

TIP #52

Don't wear makeup

Save money and protect your health. Many of the ingredients in skin care products cause cancer. If you have the habit of wearing conventional make-up every day, that could add up to almost five pounds of extra chemicals your body is absorbing every year.

What are all those chemicals doing to your health? Live longer and healthier while saving money! No more makeup!

"Life is really simple, but we insist on making it complicated."

- Confucius

TIP #53

Don't buy bottles of water

Purify your drinking water by filtering it or boiling it. And make your own water bottle that will last your lifetime and for generations to come -- a boda bag!

Boda bags are from Spain where shepherds have enjoyed liquid refreshment that they could sling over their shoulder.

Using a boda bag produces absolutely no trash. No more plastic bottles cluttering up the countryside. No more plastic chemicals leaching into your precious body and doing who-knows-what. No more industrial mining for metals to make a stainless steel water bottle.

Here in the Andes it seems the historical water bottle was a ceramic vessel with a string.

In my quest to find ways to live more simply, more in harmony with the Pachamama (and save money in the process), the boda bag resonates with my heart. It just plain feels good to imagine making and using a boda bag.

For more info on how to make a boda bag, you can check out these websites: http://www.ehow.com/how_7630580_make-bota-bags.html and http://www.ehow.com/how_7553705_harvest-pine-resin.html

"I have learned by some experience, by many examples, and by the writings of countless others before me, also occupied in the search, that certain environments, certain modes of life, certain rules of conduct are more conducive to inner and outer harmony than others. There are, in fact, certain roads that one may follow. Simplification of life is one of them."

- Ann Morrow Lindbergh

TIP #54

Make your own soap

You've probably noticed that some of these money saving tips require using soap. If you've wondered how to make your own soap, here is a basic recipe.

Tools: (These tools are now your soap-making tools. Never use them for cooking food)

- Plastic pitcher with secure lid. Label it with a skull and crossbones and the word "LYE."
- Thermometer
- Scale (in ounces)
- Stirring stick
- Rubber gloves
- Goggles or Safety Glasses
- Dust mask
- Long sleeved shirt, pants, shoes, socks, cap or scarf
- Apron
- Pot (stainless steel or enamel. Remember, this is now ONLY your soap-making pot. It will no longer be safe for food)

- Rags and towel or blanket
- Mold(s) for pouring soap into (I use old plastic deli containers)
- Heat source (stove or a really hot summer day)
- Fresh air (best to work outside so you don't breathe the fumes)
- Plastic bag for ice cubes (optional)
- Extra plastic containers for weighing ingredients

Ingredients (inspired by Dave Fisher at about.com):

- 6.5 oz. palm oil
- 6.5 oz. coconut oil
- 7.5 oz. olive oil
- 1.3 oz. castor oil
- 8 oz. distilled water
- 3.1 oz. lye (sodium hydroxide or potassium hydroxide. Sold at some hardware stores as a drain cleaner. Be sure it is pure, with no extra ingredients. It needs to be 100% solid lye crystals)
- 1 oz. essential oil fragrance (optional)
- Ice cubes (optional)
- Salt (optional)

Mix the Lye Solution:

Important Tips & Warnings

Lye is dangerous, if not handled properly. When added to water it forms poisonous vapors. Those vapors can damage your respiratory system and eyes. According to the State of Delaware's Division of Public Health some people have even gone blind from exposure to lye vapors. So, it's best to go outdoors to mix your lye. Don't do it indoors.

The United States Center for Disease Control (CDC) website has this to say about lye (as you recall, lye is another name for potassium hydroxide and also sodium hydroxide).

> Potassium hydroxide is corrosive to tissues. The health hazards of potassium hydroxide are similar to those of the other strong alkalies, such as sodium hydroxide. These substances gelatinize

tissue on contact, causing deep, painful lesions. Dust or mist exposures may cause eye or respiratory system irritation and nasal septum lesions.

Now that you know lye can gelatinize you, be sure to wear your rubber gloves, goggles, dust mask, a long sleeved shirt, shoes and socks, a cap to cover your hair, an apron and long pants. If you do happen to get any lye on you, flush with lots of water and go to a doctor immediately.

To see an instructional video on mixing lye, you can check out http://video.about.com/candleandsoap/Safely-Make-Lye-Solution.htm.

Now, let's make soap.

1. Read the instructions. Gather tools and ingredients. Put on all of your safety gear: shoes, socks, pants, long sleeved shirt, apron, cap, goggles, dust mask and rubber gloves.
2. (Optional) Put ice cubes in your plastic bag, seal it, and set it to one side to use later.
3. Weigh your solid oils, then put them in your pot. Heat to 100 degrees Fahrenheit. (On a hot day, my black enamel pot works great with just sunshine to melt my oils and keep them between 100 and 110 degrees Fahrenheit).
4. Weigh your liquid oils and add them to the pot.
5. Turn off the heat, because now you are going to mix your lye.
6. Weigh 8 ounces of distilled water and pour it into your pitcher (the one you drew a skull and crossbones on).

7. Place one of your containers on your scale and note its weight.
8. Carefully shake 3.1 ounces of lye into your container (be careful not to get any specks on you or your clothes or work area). Then seal your lye jar, wipe it (and your work area and gloves) with a damp rag. Put the lye jar someplace where no animals or children could get into it by accident.
9. Slowly and carefully sprinkle the 3.1 oz. of lye into the 8 oz. of water in the pitcher. IMPORTANT NOTE: NEVER pour the water onto the lye, it can erupt. ONLY add the lye to water, a little bit at a time.
10. Stir carefully until the lye water looks clear.
11. The lye mixture gets hot quickly, up to around 200 degrees Fahrenheit. You can let it cool down to 100 degrees F on its own, or you can float your sealed plastic bag of ice cubes in the pitcher, to cool it down more quickly to 100 degrees Fahrenheit. (Thanks to Megan of Rain Valley Soap for the ice-bag technique!)
12. Turn on the heat and check the temperature of your oils. When both the oils and the lye are between 100 to 110 degrees, slowly pour your pitcher of lye water into your pot of oils. Keep the heat at this temperature.
13. Stir continuously until the mixture thickens enough that you can see the patterns and marks of your stirrings (light trace). This can take a LONG time. Be patient, and stir carefully. Don't splash.

14. (Optional) When you see the marks of your stirring (light trace), it is time to stir in your optional fragrance essential oil.
15. (Optional) To make a harder bar of soap (with a gritty feel), you can stir in up to 10 ounces of salt at this point.
16. Pour your soap into your mold(s). (I use plastic deli containers for molds).
17. Wrap your molds in towels or blankets, so they cool slowly.
18. In about 12-24 hours (or sooner if you added salt), your soap will be hard enough to take out of the molds and to cut with a knife. (Wear your gloves!) Cut the soap like you would a hard cheese -- very carefully.
19. Store your soap for about a month to let the lye finish its chemical reactions so the soap suds will have a pH of 7 to 10. The storage time is called "curing."

Have fun!

For more info on lye and soap making you can check out *The Everything Soapmaking Book: Learn How to Make Soap at Home with Recipes, Techniques, and Step-by-Step Instructions - Purchase the right equipment ... and sell your creations*, by Alicia Grosso. There's even an online community of "soapers" you can learn from at https://www.facebook.com/soaping101.

"Simplicity is the ultimate sophistication."

- Leonardo da Vinci

TIP #55

Stop buying antiperspirants or deodorants

Soap and water will do the job. Or try a pinch of baking soda mixed into water as your natural deodorant. Some people like to use witch hazel. (See Tip #64)

Save money. Save our Pachamama from more plastic packaging in the landfill, or the energy burned and pollution caused by the process of recycling plastic. And save your health. Anything you put on your skin goes into your bloodstream.

You may even get healthier and have lower medical bills, as well as saving money now.

"Any intelligent fool can make things bigger, more complex, and more violent. It takes a touch of genius—and a lot of courage—to move in the opposite direction."

- E. F. Schumacker

TIP #56

Make your own shampoo

Did you know that shampoos you buy at the store almost always contain ingredients that cause cancer? You can save money now and in the long run if you stop buying shampoo and make your own.

The easiest and cheapest shampoo recipe I found was to add 1 tablespoon of baking soda to one cup of warm water. Stir until the powder dissolves, then use immediately.

A detangling leave-in conditioner recipe is: add one or two tablespoons of apple cider vinegar per one cup of water. To cut the odor of the vinegar you can add a sprig of rosemary or just about anything else that is edible, natural and smells good to you. Pour the liquid over your head and massage it into your scalp with your fingers.

"Man is an over-complicated organism. If he is doomed to extinction he will die out for want of simplicity."

- Ezra Pound

TIP #57

Make your own toothpaste and mouthwash

Baking soda, or just plain water, is what I use for brushing my teeth.

A toothpaste recipe you might like to try is: 1 teaspoon baking soda, 1/4 teaspoon hydrogen peroxide and 1 drop peppermint oil.

You probably already know this, but I was surprised to learn that the plaque that builds up on our teeth is really a bacterial infection rampant in Western Industrialized Society. It's been said that cultures that never ate refined sugar or processed foods do not have dental plaque.

A plaque-controlling mouthwash recipe is half water and half hydrogen peroxide. ***Don't swallow it.*** Just swish it around in your mouth for at least a minute. Then spit it out and rinse out your mouth with water.

And be sure to floss!

For more info you can check out the book *Where There Is No Dentist* by Murray Dickenson.

". . . When basic needs have been met,

human development is primarily about being *more,*

not having *more."*

- Preamble to the Earth Charter

TIP #58

Make your own lotion

The basic ingredients in lotions aren't very expensive. What is taking the money out of your pocket are: packaging, distribution and advertising. You can make lotions for yourself and even sell them! Save money and maybe also have a new source of income.

To get started, here is a recipe you can whip up in your kitchen.

Moisturizer

Ingredients

* 2 tbs. beeswax

* 1/2 c. oil (any yummy oil, or blend of oils -- almond, olive, whatever)

* distilled water

* essential oil (optional fragrance of your choice)

Directions

1. In a pot on low heat, stir constantly as you melt the beeswax into the oil(s).
2. Remove from heat, keep stirring, and slowly add distilled water until the mixture is the consistency that you want.
3. Stir in a few drops of an essential oil (optional).
4. Spoon into jars and label.

"To be a philosopher is not merely to have subtle thoughts, nor even to found a school, but to so love wisdom as to live according to its dictates a life of simplicity, independence, magnanimity and trust."

- Henry David Thoreau

TIP #59

Make your own glycerin for skin care products

You may be wondering if you can make glycerin, which is one of the ingredients in many skin care recipes. If you don't mind working with caustic lye, here is a recipe for vegetable glycerin from Kay Miranda of www.eHow.com. *Be sure and follow the safety precautions of wearing goggles and rubber gloves.*

Ingredients:

- 1 cup coconut oil
- 1 cup olive oil
- 2 tablespoons lye
- 1 cup water
- 1/2 cup salt

Special Tools:

- cooking thermometer
- safety goggles and rubber gloves

Instructions:

1. Put on safety goggles and rubber gloves.
2. In a saucepan carefully combine all of the ingredients (making sure not to splash any of that corrosive lye on you or anything else!)
3. Stir gently as you slowly heat everything to 125 degrees Fahrenheit.
4. Turn down the heat and keep stirring until the temperature drops to 100 degrees Fahrenheit.
5. At 100 degrees, keep stirring for another 15 minutes or more until the mixture thickens.
6. Remove from heat, stir in 1/2 cup of salt, then let it cool.
7. When cool, it naturally separates. There's a layer of soap on top (Yay! Bonus soap!) and glycerin on the bottom. Skim off the soap and pour it into a soap mold.
8. Store the glycerin in an airtight glass bottle or jar in the refrigerator (for up to 3 or 4 weeks).

Tips & Warnings

Lye can lead to alkali burns. Store lye in a cool dry place and always use safety gear when working with it, to prevent direct contact with skin and eyes. If contact occurs, flush the area with water and seek medical attention immediately.

"Simplicity makes me happy."

- Alicia Keys

TIP #60

Make your own sunscreen lotion

Have you ever wondered how to make your own sunscreen lotion? It might save you money. And you might also choose to sell it and have a new income stream. Here are two recipes.

Recipe #1

(from www.ehow.com)

Tools

- Double boiler
- Handheld mixer
- Storage jar
- Rubber gloves and dust mask

Ingredients

- 2 1/2 oz. sesame oil
- 1 1/2 oz. coconut oil
- 1/2 oz. beeswax
- 1/2 cup distilled water

- 2 tbsp. of zinc oxide
- 1 tbsp. wheat germ oil
- 10 to 20 drops antiseptic essential oil (optional)
- 1 tsp. vitamin C powder (or pulverize some vitamin C tablets between two metal spoons)
- 200 IU vitamin A (prick a Vitamin A gel cap with a pin and squish out whatever amount seems like it might be close to 200 IU)

Instructions

1. Put some tap water in the bottom part of your double boiler.
2. Put the sesame oil, coconut oil and beeswax in the top of the double boiler, stir together and melt over medium heat.
3. Remove from heat and pour in the distilled water.
4. Stir it all together until the consistency is smooth.
5. (Make sure you are wearing your dust mask) Add zinc oxide, wheat germ oil, vitamin C and vitamin A.
6. Drop in essential oils--if desired--and blend well.
7. Cool.
8. Spoon into a jar and seal it with a tight lid.
9. You can sell your homemade sunblock, share it with your friends or smear it on your own skin. Just be sure to use it up within six months.

Tips

You can mix in some rose water, aloe vera gel and glycerin for a smoother texture.

Recipe #2

You'll notice that this ingredient list is much shorter. The instructions are the same as for the recipe above.

Ingredients

- 8 oz. olive, sunflower, jojoba or soybean oil
- 1oz beeswax
- 2 tbsp. zinc oxide or titanium dioxide
- Optional -- Essential oils of your choice

"The little things are infinitely the most important."

- Arthur Conan Doyle

TIP #61

Make your own lip balm

Homemade natural lip balm is good for your health, and you can use it for bartering, giving as gifts or even selling for money.

Here's a recipe:

- 1 oz. Olive oil
- 0.3 oz. Lanolin (See Tip #62)
- 0.4 oz. Shea butter
- 0.4 oz. Beeswax
- (Optional) Essential oil and stevia

1. Melt the beeswax, lanolin and shea butter in a double boiler over medium heat.
2. Remove from heat and add the olive oil.
3. Stir until well mixed.
4. If you want it flavored, add a few drops of a yummy essential oil and some stevia to taste.
5. Pour into a container, let cool and seal with a cap.

"Three Rules of Work: Out of clutter find simplicity; From discord find harmony; In the middle of difficulty lies opportunity."

- Albert Einstein

TIP #62

Sell and/or use the lanolin from your sheep's wool

Free skin care lotion is walking around on the wool of your sheep. Lanolin is great, all by itself, for soothing dry or chapped skin. Some midwives recommend that nursing mothers rub their nipples with lanolin. And when you mix lanolin with other ingredients, you can make a wide variety of skin care products.

Did you know that up to a quarter of the weight of freshly shorn wool is lanolin? According to Wikipedia you can get about 250-300 ml of lanolin from the wool of one Merino sheep. Here's one way to do it.

1. Shear the sheep
2. Boil the wool in water (with some salt) for a few hours, until most of the water has boiled away.
3. Filter out the wool and any other un-dissolved solid matter from the hot solution.
4. Let the solution cool.

5. You should now be able to see a pale-yellow waxy solid coating the surface of the water. This is crude lanolin.
6. Skim off the crude lanolin and put it in a jar with some olive oil and water.
7. Screw the lid securely onto the jar and shake well until the impurities dissolve into the oil and water and you see a solid layer of off-white lanolin form between the layers of oil and water.
8. Discard the water and oil, and your lanolin is ready to use or sell or barter!

"You know you've achieved perfection in design, not when you have nothing more to add, but when you have nothing more to take away."

- Antoine de Saint-Exupery

TIP #63

Make your own lanolin hand cream

Save money by not buying any more fancy shmancy hand creams. You can make your own!

Straight lanolin (see Tip #62) is a great hand cream. But sometimes you, or your friends who you barter with, might prefer a lighter moisturizer.

Here is a recipe you may like to whip up in your kitchen.

Ingredients

- 3 Tbsp. lanolin
- 3 Tbsp. distilled water
- 3 Tbsp. grated beeswax
- 1/2 cup almond oil
- 3 Tbsp. witch hazel (See Tip #64)
- 1/8 tsp. borax powder

Directions

1. Mix the beeswax, lanolin and almond oil in a double boiler and heat just enough to make them melt into liquid.
2. Remove from heat.

3. In a saucepan, combine the witch hazel, borax powder and distilled water.
4. Stir occasionally over medium heat until you see the mixture start to boil.
5. Remove from heat and drizzle it into the double boiler, stirring constantly until well mixed .
6. Let cool.
7. (Optional) Add scent. 1 to 3 drops of an essential/aromatherapy oil per ounce of skin cream.

"Problems can not be solved at the same level of awareness that created them."

- Albert Einstein

TIP #64

Make your own Witch Hazel

Peji, my Lakota teacher, taught me that Witch Hazel is a great astringent for healing our skin. Isn't it great? Mother Nature provides all that we need!

The stuff for sale in the store is distilled with alcohol and might include other chemical ingredients. But you can make your own Witch Hazel the Native American way! Good for relieving inflammation and bruising. Here's a couple of simple recipes.

Recipe #1 (Menominee)

1. Pick some leaves off of a Witch Hazel bush.
2. Boil them in water.
3. Let cool.

4. Rub the liquid on your body wherever your muscles or joints are sore.

Recipe #2 (Mohawk)

1. Steep Witch Hazel bark like you would to make tea.
2. Let cool to room temperature.
3. You can use it as an eyewash, or soak a clean cloth as a compress.

NOTE: One commercial eyewash that is based on Witch Hazel suggests that you use fresh solution for washing each eye. Also, take out your contact lenses before rinsing your eyes with Witch Hazel, and leave the contacts out for some time (like for overnight).

Some other names for the Witch Hazel plant are: *hamamelis virginiana,* spotted adler, snapping hazel nut, and winter bloom.

For more information you can check out: Weiner, Michael A. *Earth Medicine-Earth Foods: Plant Remedies, Drugs, and Natural Foods of the North American Indians*. New York: Macmillan, 1972; and Hutchens, Alma R. *A Handbook of Native American Herbs*. Boston: New York, 1992; and Weslager, C A. *Magic Medicines of the Indians*. Somerset, N.J: Middle Atlantic Press, 1973.

"Simplicity, simplicity, simplicity!

. . . We are happy in proportion to

the things we can do without."

- Henry David Thoreau

TIP #65

Make your own house paint

Save money! Don't buy paint; make your own. It's natural and nontoxic. Here are a couple of recipes to get you started. The first is from a Quechua man who grew up herding sheep barefoot in Cajamarca, Peru. This is how his community painted the adobe walls of their homes.

1. Grind up San Pedro cactus with your *batán* stone mortar and pestle.
2. Separate the juice from the fiber.
3. Grind some earth that is the color you like.
4. Mix the earth powder into the San Pedro cactus juice. Paint on wall. Nontoxic, natural.

If you don't have lots of San Pedro cactuses around to mash up as paint binder, here's an easy recipe adapted from Mother Earth News. You can cook up paint in your kitchen. It's kind of like making a rue or gravy!

Ingredients (Makes 1 1/2 quarts)

- 1 cup flour
- 5 1/2 cups cold water
- 1 1/2 cup screened powdered clay
- pigment

Directions

1. Slowly sift flour into 2 cups cold water in a bowl, beating constantly to prevent lumps. Set aside.
2. In a large saucepan, boil 1 1/2 cups of water.
3. Turn heat low and stir constantly as you add the bowl of flour water from Step 1 to the saucepan.
4. Keep stirring over low heat until thick.
5. Remove from heat.
6. Stir in 2 cups of water, a little at a time, to thin the paste.
7. Put on a dust mask.
8. In a separate work bowl, combine the powdered clay with the pigment.
9. Slowly stir in the powder mixture, until your paint is the thickness you want.

Did you know that there are potentially 300 toxic chemicals and 150 carcinogens in oil-based paint? That's what a John Hopkins University study found.

Save money now by making your own natural paint. And you can save money in the long run on health care by using natural paint in your home.

For more info you can check *The Natural Paint Book* by Lynn Edwards and Julia Lawless.

"Simplicity is the most difficult thing to secure in this world; it is the last limit of experience and the last effort of genius."

- George Sand

TIP #66

Don't buy Drano

Remember that saying, "An ounce of prevention is worth a pound of cure?" Why wait until the drain is clogged? Putting a strainer over the drain will catch the big stuff. And you can keep grease out of the drain by wiping it off the pots and pans before you wash them.

But if your drain does get clogged with grease, you can try de-greasing it by pouring ½ cup of baking soda into the drain, then pour in 1 cup of vinegar. Let it bubble for about 15 minutes, then rinse it out with boiling water. If the clog is bad, repeat the process as many times as needed.

Save money, protect Pachamama and your own health by not using toxic (and expensive) chemicals.

"The poor of the world can not be helped by mass production, only by production by the masses."

- Gandhi

TIP #67

Don't buy canned food

Save money in the long run on health care costs -- don't buy canned food. Did you know that the epoxy resin used to line almost all food cans contains bisphenol-A (BPA)? BPA is linked to hormone disruption, obesity, heart disease, and much more.

Instead of canned food, you can eat fresh food from your community garden (see Tip #21), dried food (see Tip #23) or jarred foods (see Tip #24).

"The whole is simpler than the sum of its parts."

- Willard Gibbs

TIP #68

Don't buy pesticides

Keep your plants well fed with compost, or all that excellent free fertilizer your sheep is producing (see Tip #30). Your plants will be stronger and healthier to resist those pests. We are more immune to disease when we practice good nutrition; the same is true of our vegetable gardens.

Pesticides, on the other hand, not only kill pests, they are also extremely toxic to all living things -- including us. Residual poisons can contaminate air, linger on surfaces and get tracked into the house on the bottom of your shoes.

Be healthier and save money!

For more info you can check out www.BeyondPesticides.com and the organic gardening books by Eliot Coleman.

"'Don't be dependent on anyone' -- that is my sentiment. We each have to strengthen and develop ourselves through our own efforts. We must never surrender to any foe or difficulty. We must be fearless. This is the true spirit of self-reliance."

- Daisaku Ikeda

(page 151, For Today and Tomorrow)

TIP #69

Don't go to the dry cleaners

Most clothes that say "Dry Clean Only" do just fine if you wash them by hand in cold water with gentle soap. Squeeze the water out gently and lay the clothing out flat to dry. You not only save money right away, you also protect your health.

Did you know that a Consumer Reports' study showed that habitually wearing clothes that have been freshly dry cleaned can increase your risk of cancer by 150? Not to mention causing nervous system, kidney, liver and reproductive disorders. And you raise the level of the carcinogen perchloroethylene in your home for up to a week whenever you hang a newly dry cleaned garment in the closet. Breath tests show that even walking into a dry cleaning establishment will about double the amount of perchloroethylene in your system.

"So what" if our clothes aren't perfect. Better to be healthy and maybe a bit rumpled, I say, than being the finest-dressed corpse you've ever seen.

For more info you can check out http://healthychild.org/blog/comments/greenwashing_how_to_dry_clean_only_without_perc#ixzz1sQpBdeE5.

"I believe we would be happier to have a personal revolution in our individual lives and go back to simpler living and more direct thinking. It is the simple things of life that make living worthwhile, the sweet fundamental things such as love and duty, work and rest, and living close to nature."

- Laura Ingalls Wilder

TIP #70

Don't buy moth balls

Save flowers from the lavender bush you planted in your community garden (see Tip #21). You can gather the lavender flowers into little bundles and put them with your woolen clothes and blankets. Did you know that lavender sachets ward off moths? Saves you money at the check out stand, and at the doctor's office, since you won't be breathing that nasty chemical naphthalene.

For more info you can check out www.healthychild.org.

" . . . Women could break with the old male-centered civilization of power and build a new civilization founded on cooperation and reciprocity like the all-fulfilling force of life."

-Daisaku Ikeda

TIP #71

Don't buy perfumes or colognes

Save money by not buying perfumes or colognes. Not only your bank account, but your health will thank you. Did you know that lots of fragrances contain hundreds of chemicals including the "secret ingredient" diethyl phthalate? DEP is a suspected carcinogen and hormone disruptor that is linked to reproductive disorders. Even if you buy perfume cheap at the 99 Cent Store, getting cancer is a big bummer that will not save you money.

For more info you can check out www.healthychild.org.

"A little simplification would be the first step toward rational living, I think."

- Eleanor Roosevelt

TIP #72

White vinegar to the rescue

White vinegar. That is what we used for sanitizing when I helped out in the kitchen of Occupy Portland, Oregon.

Spraying full strength vinegar on wood will also kill dry rot spores.

Another use of white vinegar is for eliminating odors from pet "accidents." A suggested recipe is 1 part vinegar to 4 parts water.

White vinegar and water is also good for mopping floors and surfaces. It's a good idea to test the surface first to make sure the vinegar will not damage it.

White vinegar. It's cheaper than other cleaners. And best of all, it's natural -- protecting your health so you have a better chance of having more days of life to enjoy with wonderful friends on our beautiful Mother Earth.

3 Bonus Tips on How to Survive a Tsunami

1. Listen to your Elders

Did you know that while thousands were swept to their deaths and entire communities destroyed in the tsunami of December 26, 2004, the five indigenous tribes on neighboring Andaman and Nicobar islands in the Indian archipelago were fine?

Why was that? They listened to their elders.

For generations, going back as far as 70,000 years, these people have learned to listen to nature as intimately as listening to a lover. The children learn from the elders how to develop this "ear." The people knew the tsunami was coming so everyone went to high ground.

Unlike a Canadian couple who stood on a resort beach snapping photos of the 2004 tsunami. A photo of that tsunami, later downloaded from the seawater-soaked chip of their camera, was found with their corpses. I am deeply saddened and angered at a society that teaches people that nature is an object to be consumed. That consumer value system, in my opinion, murdered this couple.

2. Don't Develop / Destroy your Coastline

Live at least 10 km inland. That is the rule of thumb of these wise people, the Great Andamanese, Onges, Jarawas, Sentinelese and Shompens. Unlike their neighbors, they did not cut down the trees growing on the coastline.

Their Western-style neighbors clear-cut in order to build luxury hotels and make expanses of sandy beaches for frolicking tourists. The trees are what hold it all together. Those photo-op sandy beaches on other islands turned into tourist cemeteries.

Living in harmony with nature is more important, to these indigenous people, than being part of a "modern" tourist consumer economy.

3. Help Each Other

Rather than dreaming of living secluded in your own Malibu beach house, clinging to a cliff with a security guard at the gate -- form community. Get to know your neighbors. Help each other out. Mutual aid is scientifically proven to be the way for survival of the species. These true survivors, the Great Andamanese, Onges, Jarawas, Sentinelese and Shompens, live in egalitarian hunter/gatherer societies. They lived while thousands died.

We can learn from indigenous wisdom and try to incorporate it into our lives, bit by bit.

Afterword

As fellow travelers on paths of deepening our awareness that "We are one," and living in more sustainable ways in equilibrium with our Mother, the Earth -- Pachamama, I thank you for having taken the time to read my book *72 Money Saving Tips for the 99%.*

If this book has peaked your interest in changing the world by living more simply and being authentically "you," you may enjoy reading some of the practical, inspiring, and/or thought-provoking books listed on the next pages.

Suggested Reading

- *1491: New Revelations of the Americas Before Columbus,* Charles C. Mann, Vintage, New York, 2006
- *Buddhism Day by Day; Wisdom for Modern Life,* Daisaku Ikeda, Middleway Press, 2006
- *Caprine Supply's Goatkeeping 101: Sensible Information From People Who Know and Raise Goats*, Caprine Supply, 1999
- *The Complete Tightwad Gazette*, Amy Dacyczyn, Villard/Random House, 1998
- *Encyclopedia of Country Living,* Carla Emery, Sasquatch Books, 2008
- *The Foxfire Book; Hog Dressing, Log Cabin Building, Mountain Crafts and Foods, Planting by the Signs, Snake Lore, Hunting Tales, Faith Healing, Moonshining, and Other Affairs of Plain Living,* Eliot Wigginton, Anchor, 1972 (There are 12 volumes)
- *For Today & Tomorrow; Daily encouragement,* Daisaku Ikeda, World Tribune Press, 2006
- *Four Arguments for the Elimination of Television*, Jerry Mander, William Marrow Paperbacks, 1978

- *Four Ways of Being Human*, Gene Lisitzky, Viking, 1956
- *Great Cosmic Mother; Rediscovering the religion of the earth,* Monica Sjoo and Barbara Mor, HarperOne, 2nd edition, 1987
- *How to Stay Alive in the Woods,* Bradford Angier, Black Dog and Leventhal Publishers, 2001
- *Indian Herbology of North America,* Almar Hutchens, Shambhala, 1991
- *The Life of Mahatma Gandhi,* Louis Fischer, Harper Collins, 2004
- *Mutual Aid; A Factor of Evolution*, Petr Kropotkin, University of Michigan Library, 1917
- *The Natural Paint Book*, Lynn Edwards and Julia Lawless, Rodale Books, 2003
- *No Logo*, Naomi Klein, Picador, New York, 2009
- *People's History of the United States*, Howard Zinn, Harper Collins, New York, 2010
- *Planetary Citizenship; Your values, beliefs and actions can shape a sustainable world*, Hazel Henderson and Daisaku Ikeda, Middleway Press, Santa Monica, California, 2004
- *Propaganda,* Edward Bernays, 1928
- *Respect the Spindle,* Abby Franquemont, Interweave Press, 2009

- *The Secret Life of Plants*, Peter Tompkins and Christopher Bird, Harper Perennial, 1989
- *The Shock Doctrine; The rise of disaster capitalism,* Naomi Klein, Picador, 2008
- *Small is Beautiful; Economics as if People Mattered,* E.F. Schumacher, Harper Perennial (Reprint Edition), 2010
- *Up From Slavery*, Booker T. Washington, Tribeca, New York, 2012
- *Walden*, Henry David Thoreau, Dover, 1995
- *Where There is No Dentist;* Murray Dickenson, Hesperian Foundation, 1983
- *Where There is No Doctor; a village healthcare handbook,* David Werner, Jane Maxwell, Carol Thuman; Hesperian Foundation, 1992
- *Wild Edible Plants of Western North America,* Donald R. Kirk, Naturegraph, 1970, 1975
- *The Winter Gardening Handbook; Year Round Vegetable Production Using Deep Organic Techniques and Unheated Greenhouses,* Eliot Coleman, Chelsea Green Publishing, 2009
- *Writings of Nichiren Daishonin,* Gosho Translation Committee, Soka Gakkai, 1999 (There are two volumes)

Write your own Tips here

www.ingramcontent.com/pod-product-compliance
Lightning Source LLC
Chambersburg PA
CBHW072237270326
41930CB00010B/2162
9780984375653